Mehari Fisseha

Responsibility to Protect: Humanitarian Intervention in Africa

Case study – Darfur

Anchor Academic
Publishing

Fisseha, Mehari: Responsibility to Protect: Humanitarian Intervention in Africa. Case study – Darfur, Hamburg, Anchor Academic Publishing 2016

Buch-ISBN: 978-3-95489-471-0
PDF-eBook-ISBN: 978-3-95489-971-5
Druck/Herstellung: Anchor Academic Publishing, Hamburg, 2016

Bibliografische Information der Deutschen Nationalbibliothek:
Die Deutsche Nationalbibliothek verzeichnet diese Publikation in der Deutschen Nationalbibliografie; detaillierte bibliografische Daten sind im Internet über http://dnb.d-nb.de abrufbar.

Bibliographical Information of the German National Library:
The German National Library lists this publication in the German National Bibliography. Detailed bibliographic data can be found at: http://dnb.d-nb.de

All rights reserved. This publication may not be reproduced, stored in a retrieval system or transmitted, in any form or by any means, electronic, mechanical, photocopying, recording or otherwise, without the prior permission of the publishers.

Das Werk einschließlich aller seiner Teile ist urheberrechtlich geschützt. Jede Verwertung außerhalb der Grenzen des Urheberrechtsgesetzes ist ohne Zustimmung des Verlages unzulässig und strafbar. Dies gilt insbesondere für Vervielfältigungen, Übersetzungen, Mikroverfilmungen und die Einspeicherung und Bearbeitung in elektronischen Systemen.

Die Wiedergabe von Gebrauchsnamen, Handelsnamen, Warenbezeichnungen usw. in diesem Werk berechtigt auch ohne besondere Kennzeichnung nicht zu der Annahme, dass solche Namen im Sinne der Warenzeichen- und Markenschutz-Gesetzgebung als frei zu betrachten wären und daher von jedermann benutzt werden dürften.

Die Informationen in diesem Werk wurden mit Sorgfalt erarbeitet. Dennoch können Fehler nicht vollständig ausgeschlossen werden und die Diplomica Verlag GmbH, die Autoren oder Übersetzer übernehmen keine juristische Verantwortung oder irgendeine Haftung für evtl. verbliebene fehlerhafte Angaben und deren Folgen.

Alle Rechte vorbehalten

© Anchor Academic Publishing, Imprint der Diplomica Verlag GmbH
Hermannstal 119k, 22119 Hamburg
http://www.diplomica-verlag.de, Hamburg 2016
Printed in Germany

Abstract

The atrocities in Darfur pose crucial challenges in legal and policy frameworks in both the regional and international front, particularly in the areas of addressing state sovereignty and ensuring human security for those who are caught up in armed conflict. This dissertation is about exploring the doctrine of Responsibility to Protect (R2P) with focus on the role on the international community in protecting civilians in armed conflict, especially in Darfur. The research question being investigated by this research is premised on analysing the current situation in Darfur in light of the R2P doctrine. This research's scope will be on the legal framework that created the R2P doctrine, what informed its formation, the status of the international community with regard to humanitarian intervention, the situation in Darfur, the flaws of the R2P principle and justification for change in the same if international intervention is to successfully work. The international community lacks political will, it is faced by logistical obstacles and political maneuver. On the other hand part of the international community often leads to more tragedies that it intended to curb. For R2P to be successfully implemented towards civilian protection, several conditions need to simultaneously take place. They include the existence of one of the 4 mass atrocities that spur R2P, adequate and reliable capabilities to react, the readiness of the international community to risk the lives of their soldiers to go and protect non-citizens, and the unavailability of the necessary preparation and concepts to address the particular necessities of the conflict environment that are non-permissive. Since its September 2005 inception, there are several strains in the R2P principle that remains unresolved to date. This needs to be considered when assessing the unavailability of answers to issues of how the international community and global leaders ought to have responded since 2003, when the Darfur armed conflict began.

List of Abbreviations

AU – African Union

ICC – International Criminal Court

ICG – International Crisis Group

ICISS – International Commission on Intervention and State Sovereignty

IHL – International Humanitarian Law

JEM – Justice and Equality Movement

LNTS – League of Nations Treaty Series

NATO – North Atlantic Treaty Organisation

OAU – Organisation of African Unity

R2P – Responsibility to Protect

SLM – Sudan Liberation Movement

SLM-MM – Sudan Liberation Movement Minni Minnawi

SPLM –N – Sudan People Liberation Movement North

SRF – Sudan Revolutionary Front

UN - United Nations

UNAMID – African Union-United Nations Missions in Darfur

UNOCHA – United Nations Office for the Coordination of Humanitarian Affairs

US – United States

Table of contents

Abstract 7

List of Abbreviations 9

Table of contents 11

CHAPTER 1 – INTRODUCTION 13
   1.1 Historical background 14
   1.2 Rationale of the study 15
   1.3 Aims and objectives 17
   1.4 Structure of the dissertation 17

CHAPTER 2 – LITERATURE REVIEW 19
   2.1 The international community and protecting civilians in armed conflict 19
      2.1.1 Inadequate political will 20
      2.1.2 Logistical obstacles 21
         2.1.2.1 Moral Hazard 22
   2.2 The case of Darfur 24
   2.3 The protection of Civilians and R2P 26

CHAPTER 3 – METHODOLOGY 29
   3.1 Research Approach 29
   3.2 Reliability and Validity 30
   3.3 Analysis of UN documentation on R2P in the context of Darfur 31
      3.3.1 Legal Objections to Humanitarian Intervention 31
      3.3.2 Impasse in reconciling state sovereignty and humanitarian intervention 32
      3.3.3 Tackling the legal objections 33
   3.4 Roles and limitations of the International Criminal Court in internal conflict 34

CHAPTER 4 – THE NEED TO CHANGE THE ROLE OF THE INTERNATIONAL COMMUNITY IN DARFUR 37
   4.1 Failure of R2P in Darfur 37
   4.2 Selective State practice 38
      4.2.1 Interest-Based Selectivity 38
      4.2.2 Racial-based selectivity 39
   4.3 Inadequate Humanitarian Discourse 40
   4.4 Review of documentary evidence regarding the process of intervention 41

CHAPTER 5 – CONCLUSION AND RECOMMENDATION 44
    5.1   Conclusion 44
    5.2   Recommendations 45

Appendix 47

Bibliography 49

CHAPTER 1 – INTRODUCTION

Human rights are a key element in global politics and legal frameworks. The United Nations, agrees that human rights are important in the governance of people. Unfortunately, the world has experienced, over time, many instances of human rights violations. The violations are committed through war, genocides, crimes against humanity, forceful eviction of persons, discrimination, and living in deplorable conditions among others. Ideally, governments are supposed to ensure that rights of their people are respected. However, some governments especially in developing nations have subjugated the rule of law to protect human rights. Some have been passive, allowed violations of human rights to happen, while others have actually propagated violation of human rights. Some of the issues of human rights have been recorded in Rwanda, Democratic Republic of Congo, Sudan and Chad among other countries. Following the intensity of deterioration of human rights in Africa, there has been a justification for the United Nations to intervene in order to protect the rights of peoples.

According to Appiah-Mensah (2006) close to 10 years after the Rwandan Genocide and several meetings of finding a way forward, the response to the Darfur conflicts from the international community that started in 2003, seemed to be a case of déjà vu. The world just watched in apathy and shock as the Arab dominated government of Sudan facilitated ethnical cleansing in the vast Darfur region by assisting Arab militia with arms and air support to continue maiming, killing and raping black Africans. Bach (2008) asserted that the situation in Darfur is a combination of the worst crimes: sexual assault, armed conflict, extreme violence, internally displaced persons. He contended that the evidence at hand makes the situation reminiscent of the German Holocaust. Bellamy, Williams and Griffin (2004) contend that the violence in Darfur pose crucial challenges in legal and policy frameworks in both the regional and international front, particularly in the areas of addressing state sovereignty and ensuring human security for those who are caught up in armed conflict. On the global platform, the atrocities taking place in the Darfur region present dilemmas and challenges for the UNSC, which is tasked with ensuring peace and security is maintained on the international scene. It realises this through coming up with effective strategies designed to curb and eliminate threats to peace and realise international co-operation in seeking solutions to international situations of humanitarian in nature. Closer home, Darfur presents policy dilemmas and legal challenges to the AU – a creation of the Constitutive Act of 2000 to address the major issues that Africans have to deal with, promote and ensure security across

Africa (Adebajo, 2008; Woodward, 2001; Annan, 2000). The situation maligning Darfur brings to the fore the Principle of R2P or responsibility to protect, which is meant to encompass the international community's right to protect civilians caught through acts of humanitarian intervention; these civilians often end up being the victims of armed conflict. As a result, it has been agreed that in cases where human rights are grossly violated, the Security Council of the UN could take action. This principle has been referred to as Responsibility to Protect (R2P). This dissertation explores that R2P application in the case of Darfur in Sudan.

1.1 Historical background

Calls to advance the R2P grew from recognizing the inadequate reaction from the UN towards adding to the morally indefensible and grotesque mass atrocities that have taken place in the 20th century; from the Holocaust, Bosnia, Rwanda, Kosovo, Congo, Liberia, and now Darfur (Cilliers, 2008; Cilliers and Malan, 2005). In all the aforementioned situations, the international community sat by and watched as acts of violence were conducted out in brutal and systemic forms. Inaction was defended on fact that state sovereignty was far superior compared to the responsibility of the international community to protect innocent civilians who had turned into victims of war. At the entry of the 21st century, the former UN Secretary General posed to the UN member states a challenge by asserting that if intervention from the international community constituted an affront towards the sovereignty of the state, then at which stage should the international community come in with regard to responding to systemic and gross abuses of human rights that continuously afflict common humanity (Callaghy, Kassimir and Latham, 2001a). In responding to this, the Canadian government called onto the ICISS, who issued "The Responsibility to Protect" in 2001; a report that according to Collins (2008) reconceptualised the challenge posed by Annan on the point of humanitarian intervention with regard to protecting innocent civilians caught up in armed conflict by the international community. Tentatively, the report shifted the issue from the proponents of the actions to the victims of the conflict.

According to Callaghy, Kassimir and Latham, (2001b), R2P respects that the sovereign state bears the responsibility of protecting its citizenry. However, in the event that the state is either unwilling or unable so to do, then the onus in on the international community to intervene and perform the same role; this is especially the case for crimes against humanity, genocide, war crimes and ethnic cleansing. De Coning (2005a) argues that even though the biggest innovation of R2P entails altering the concept of civilian protection to a responsibility from a right and justifying military intervention as the last resort. The Principle addresses responsibility in three fronts: responsibility to rebuilt, prevent and react. This will ensure that there is lasting and sustainable peace across the world; particularly in regions there is armed conflict.

The High-Level Panel on Threats, Challenges, and Change that was formed by the Secretary General Koffi Annan in 2004 was tasked with monitoring the international community and identifying any major threats to peace and security. Thereafter, this panel was to come with policies and institutions to eliminate the threats to peace and create frameworks to deal with future events. (De Coning, 2005b). After conducting vigorous research, the panel endorsed R2P as a fundamental and emerging norm through their report "A More Secure World: Our Shared Responsibility." In addition, this report underscored the three-pronged role of the R2P as was indicated by the ICISS. In the 2005 World Summit, De Waal (2007a) asserted that all present member states conglomerated at the UN to discuss matters of development, security, partial reform in the UN, and protection of human rights. At the end of the World Summit, all the member states unanimously signed the Outcomes Document that affirmed the UN should protect populations caught up in armed conflict. The UNSC passed resolutions 1706 and 1674 that underlined the role and purpose of the R2P (De Waal, 2007b). However, despite the gleam and magnificent provisions of the R2P and affiliated documents there are still questions on how they can be applied in cases of armed conflict; particularly in the case of Darfur.

1.2 Rationale of the study

Sovereign states have the responsibility to protect its citizenry; this is the key principle in R2P. Failure to do so demands action from the international community. The R2P framework is premised in an approach to ensure that civilians are protected, but it appears that the primary objective is not to intervene, but to remove the alleged perpetrator of armed conflicts; the individual who is believed to be behind all the crimes taking place in Darfur, Al-Bashir.

At the present time two arrest warrants are in effect; as of November 2013, al-Bashir has not been arrested. While it might be argued that the ICC's actions in charging and indicting al-Bashir represent an effort of R2P, it could also be argued that the failure to arrest Bashir, particularly in the conjunction with the refusal of the Governments of Sudan, Egypt, Qatar, Djibouti and Chad to turn over Bashir to the ICC when he has been in their nations represents a supreme failure of R2P. By investigating the current situation in Darfur in light of the responsibility to protect (R2P) on analytical platform, this study will contribute to the body of evidence that can be utilised to develop the next steps for protecting civilians in Darfur in light of the armed conflict in the region. It is imperative to assess varying positions on the situation in Darfur, Western Sudan and to present a carefully considered position paper that incorporates all sides of the situation in terms of humanitarian needs and responsibility to protect the civilians in the Darfur Region.

Mehta (2009) suggests that it is time to establish language which requires specific guidance regarding the legitimate utilization of force in regard to R2P. A resolution was passed in 2005 by the UN that allows the international community to assist other nations in meeting their humanitarian obligations to care for their populations, and which allows the UN to act when the nations do not do so (United Nations, 2005). Mehta suggests that the time has come to establish the requirement for intervention, based on the concept of serious harm. This project is based on the framework of shared normative understanding concerning the military use through UNSC directive and exploring the emerging norm of legality. The ICISS determined that "the emerging norm that there is a collective international R2P, that can only be exercised by the UNSC when its authorising the use of military force as the last effort" (United Nations, 2004) but did not provide the requriement for the intervention.

The responsibility to protect (R2P) has been driven by the violation of human rights on a large scale in the last few years. Rwandan genocide, the crisis in Sierra Leone, and now in Darfur has followed on the heels of international intervention in Kosovo in 1999. The question arises as to whether or not humanitarian intervention is a norm, and whether or not the norm should be invoked by individual states, or the United Nations Security Council (Kosovo, 2000). The further issue that arises is whether intervention is a right, or a duty. If it is a duty, then the UN Security Council may be failing in that duty. Under the role of sovereignty, if we agree that the States have the primary role of protection, and then surely they have failed in that role when their leader is indicted on multiple violent charges on populations. Placed in this context, the responsibility to protect would take on a new and international importance, surely qualifying for the UN Security Council intervention "where appropriate" (United Nations Security Council, 2013, para. 1).

The R2P framework is relevant to the Darfur crisis. Darfur is an example of an unwilling and unable government to shield its citizens from the harmful effects of war, as well as unfortunately, an international community that is equally unwiling and/or incapable of embracing the soveriegn responsibility that is envisaged by the R2P. As such, it is fundamental to identify and underline the Principle of R2P and intervention of the international community in protecting civilians from being victims of armed conflict in light of the case in Darfur.

1.3 Aims and objectives

The UN has mandated the responsibility to protect (R2P). Darfur has offered particular challenges to those wishing to intervene. Humanitarian goals in Darfur are threatened. More than 300,000 have lost their lives in the Darfur conflict since rebels first began asserting independence against the Sudanese government ten years ago (Associated Press, 2012). The UNAMID peacekeeping mission in Darfur is tasked with protecting civilians, providing humanitarian aid, reconciling the political effort, and promoting human rights (Associated Press, 2012). The Sudanese Armed Forces have been conducting air strikes and more residents have recently died as the result of unidentified armed attacks, rape, and looting (Fasher, 2012).

On February 13, 2013, the United Nations Security Council reaffirmed its position that in the case of innocent civilians who are targeted in armed conflicts. States have the primary responsibility for safety (United Nations Security Council, 2013, para. 1). The Council also stated that the international community should ensure the continuation of peace-keeping missions and that these missions should have priority use of resources when needed for that purpose (United Nations Security Council, 2013, para. 1).

The aim of this research therefore is to consider what the current UN role should be in ther case of armed conflict in Darfur. The objective of the research is as hereunder;

a) To investigate the current situation in Darfur in light of the Responsibility to Protect (R2P).
b) To recommend the next steps for protecting civilians in Darfur in light of the armed conflict in the region.

1.4 Structure of the dissertation

In an effort to fully satisfy the above mentioned aims and objectives, this study will be divided into five chapters. The first chapter has been on the introduction of what the research will discuss; particularly the right to protecting innocent civilians caught up in armed conflict on the part of the international community. The second chapter will be the literature review, it will discuss the status of the international community with regard to humanitarian intervention, how it has worked and failed in previous situations, the reasons for the same, and the situation in Darfur. Chapter three will be on the methodology employed by the researcher in formulating this research, it will discuss the research approach, validity and reliability of the information acquired .The fourth chapter will highlight the flaws of the R2P principle and the justification for change in the same if international intervention is to successfully work and an in-depth analysis of documentary and the UN evidence regarding international intervention as enshrined in the principle of R2P.. The fifth chapter will be the conclusion and recommendations.

CHAPTER 2 – LITERATURE REVIEW

2.1 The international community and protecting civilians in armed conflict

The concept of the humanitarian intervention in instances of armed conflict is not a recent doctrine. It is enshrined in history as a practice and a concept (De Waal, 2007c). De Conin (2006), notes that the current historical analysis of intervention of the international community in protecting civilians illustrates a development in the concept of humanitarian intervention over time. However, Field (2004) is of the opinion that the development and actual implementation of this form of intervention has fallen victim to political circumstances and is not being moved by actual human suffering. Inasmuch as the doctrine was formulated on a premise of protecting human beings in times of armed conflict when their governments are unwilling or incapable of assisting them, the practice has evidently been failing to realise its objectives in current times. Francis, Faal, Kabia and Ramsbotham (2005) argue that the current world order is founded on contemporary principles of state security and state sovereignty has been slowing down efforts to facilitate actual humanitarian intervention urgently in times of need. Supportively, Flint and de Waal (2008) contend that other priorities are obliterating violation of human rights taking place across the world.

According to Francis (2006) even recent attempts to resuscitate the doctrine of humanitarian intervention, such as the R2P, have fallen wayward to similar state-centered traps that have again led to the failure to prioritise the life of innocent human beings, and to underpin an impartial authority tasked with the responsibility of actualizing humanitarian intervention. Grono (2006) further notes that the post 9/11 attacks have poisoned and weakened humanitarian intervention doctrine. This is because it has been integrated with the US new definitions and understandings of preemptive self defense, which politicizes the rationale of humanitarian intervention; consequently, the doctrine and its purpose has become more confusing than ever.

MacQueen (2002) notes that the international community has failed Darfur, Rwanda and other countries stifled in armed conflict resulting in the deaths and displacement of millions of civilians. Kagwanja and Mutahi (2007) add that the Rwanda genocide highlighted the unfortunate, albeit tragic, consequence of inaction and silence. The tenets of humanitarianism that have been gaining momentum ever since the Holocaust and armed conflict in Cambodia were demanded to be impartially and urgently implemented. Kent and Malan (2003) agree that at that juncture, humanitarian intervention and the R2P were found to contain serious and fundamental deficits in their implementation. Furthermore, States were seen to employ humanitarianism on a rhetorical and selective level, Johnstone, Tortolani and Gowan (2005) contend that intervention was partially seen from States that sought to protect their interests and the race of the victims. Juma (2006) further notes that such forms of selectivity were found not only be horrific, but they were also contrary to the provisions that underline the protection of human rights. The reason that the situations were facilitated, according to Ekengard (2008), was due to the dysfunction of the international organisations, and the lack of impartial authority to intervene and protect the innocent civilians. The situation in Rwanda clarified the foregoing concerns and need to address the apparent gaps in humanitarian intervention. In addition, hope and efforts were raised to curb similar humanitarian disasters from occurring. Unfortunately, this was not the case as would be underlined in the case of Darfur.

2.1.1 Inadequate political will

Civilians are the primary casualties of war across the world (Associated Press, 2012). Most of the armed conflicts taking place are within sovereign territories and they have continued unabated for many years despite attempts of international community to find solutions. However, Clough (n.d.) argues that despite the international community declaring on several occasions that it has the responsibility to protect innocent civilians in instances of armed conflict; it has lacked the political will to put a stop to the violence until it is too late when many lives have been lost. Nonetheless, Bogland, Egnell and Lagerstrom (2008) note that political will have a tendency of disintegrating amidst intervention, particularly when the forces of intervention are confronted with casualties. For example, in 1992 when the UN peacekeeping forces were deployed in Bosnia they were denied authority to intervene and protect the civilians until 1995 when more than 100,000 Bosnians had lost their lives. Similarly, Brickhill (2007) adds that in case of Somalia, the US and the UN failed to deploy military intervention till late 1992 when close to 30,000 civilians had lost their lives due to famine resulting from the armed conflict. Later, all the forces that had been deployed were later withdrawn in October 1993 after 18 US soldiers were killed. Supportively, Curtis (2001) notes that in 1994 when the Rwandan Genocide commenced, the UN quickly voted to withdraw significant portions of its peacekeeping forces as soon as 10 of them were killed on the first day. However, Fasher (2012) argues that in 2000, British peacekeeping forces successfully intervened in Sierra Leone to halt a civil war. Though this was after less willing UN and regional interventions had failed to curb the killing of tens of thousands, and commission of gruesome atrocities throughout the previous 9 years. The same case was replicated in Liberia, when regional and US peacekeepers successfully intervened in 2003 to end a civil war; although this occurred after previous attempts by regional peacekeeping forces failed to prevent the killings of tens of thousands of innocent civilians over the earlier period of 13 years of civil war.

2.1.2 Logistical obstacles

Gberie (2004) is of the opinion that even if the international community were to have the political will for robust and rapid intervention in armed conflicts, it would be extremely difficult to protect that populations at-risk since the perpetrators will always be at vantage points allowing them to act faster compared to the interveners. For example, Kagwanja and Mutahi (2007) assert that although conflict dragged on for more than 3 years in Bosnia, most of the ethnic cleansing took place in early 1992. When the Western media was arriving in the scene later in that year, two thirds of the entire republic had been occupied by the Serbian forces, and in the process more than 1 million residents had been displaced. Similarly, Krasner (2003) affirms that close to half of the Tutsi half-million victims of the Rwandan genocide were killed within the first 3 weeks of April 1994, when the genocide started. More so, when the Croatian army finally managed to broker a deal that stopped conflict that had gone on for 3 years in August 1995, Olsson (2010) argues that in less than a week it ethnically cleansed more than 100,000 Serbs who resided in the Krajina region. As well, Rankhumise (2003) notes that when Serbian forces in Kosovo abandoned their policy of counter insurgency to ethnic cleansing in March 1999, which was informed by responding to decisions from NATO to launch air strikes; in less than 2 weeks they managed to expel more than half of the ethnic Albanians residing in the province.

Moreover, later in 1999 in East Timor, after a vote for independence in a little more than a week, militias who were backed by the Indonesian government went on a rampage displacing many Timorese residents and destroying infrastructure in the province. By contrast, Raustiala (2003) affirms that even if the international community had sufficient political will, it is impossible to deploy intervention forces that are adequately equipped so quickly, and over such long distances. For instance, in August 1990 when Kuwait was invaded by Iraq's army, the US factually possessed the political will to send to Saudi Arabia, aptly equipped forces within the shortest time possible in order to protect the oil fields. The foregoing notwithstanding, the first deployment unit comprising slightly over 2,300 US troops took close to 10 days to access the region, and more than a week to adequately prepare itself to venture beyond the confines of its temporary base. Even though the US possesses the best force-projection capability across the world, and on the other hand, Saudi Arabia has a warm welcome and solid airfield infrastructure, the small force still needed more than a fortnight to ably prepare itself and deploy. Reasons for such delays, according to Presse (2012) are several, but mainly stem from three areas: the necessary equipment is very heavy, modern militaries cannot operate effectively without their equipment, and there are limits to the extents to which such equipments can be airlifted to distant and remote countries. Therefore, World Report (2012) supports the foregoing by contending that the delays could in fact be much longer for larger intervening troops, the nature of resistance that the interveners were facing, and the state of infrastructure of the deployment region.

To this end, UNOCHA (2013) argues that in the case of Rwanda, the US could have required at least 6 weeks to act and deploy task forces of more than 15,000 troops, personnel and their equipment, as soon as the genocide came to light. Furthermore, a much larger US force- similar to the ones deployed in the Dominican Republic, Haiti and Panama, would have taken a much longer period. In addition, Kushkush (2013) is of the opinion that a multi-lateral intervention would have taken a much longer time since the troop contributors do not have the US capacity to deploy rapidly. This means that by the time the international community could have realistically deployed intervention forces in Rwanda, significant portions of the targeted population would already have been annihilated. Nonetheless, Jackson (2002) frowns upon this school of thought by affirming that the fact that civil violence is actually facilitated faster than any form of intervention could arrive is not a reason for lack of intervening. The reason for this is that there is always a chance of saving some lives albeit through belated intervention. Even so, the potential to save lives through humanitarian intervention is far smaller than is often appreciated (Bolton, 2005). This is illustrated in the following section.

2.1.2.1 Moral Hazard

Mehta (2009) notes that the most counter-intuitive element of the R2P is that it may at times lead to the tragedies that it was intended to curb. The reason for this according to Natarajan (2011) is that ethnic cleansing and genocide are characterised by retaliation to the state following actions against a sub-state group for rebellion. Aboagye (2007) also notes that armed secession by some of its members could trigger the same. Therefore, the emerging norm from the point of view of Appiah-Mensah (2006) is that by raising the hopes of military and diplomatic interventions meant to protect these clusters, unintentionally facilitates rebellion through raising its chances of success and lowering its projected costs. This means that intervention at times propels rebels to realise their political goals; however, it is often always too late to avoid retaliation against civilians.Bach (2008) compares the emerging norm to an imperfect insurance policy taken against genocidal violence. A moral hazard is created that promotes risky behaviours punctuated by rebellion by the group members that are susceptible to genocidal retaliation. As well, it is impossible to fully protect civilians in these groups from the imminent backlash. This means that intervention from the international community causes genocidal violence that otherwise could not have happened in the first place.

For example, Bellamy, Williams and Griffin (2004) state that in the early 1990s, Muslim leaders in Bosnia looked for ways to secede from Yugoslavia in order to create a path for the creation of their own state, where the Muslims would enjoy from being a majority ethnic group. However, since the Muslims faced opposition from the rest of Yugoslavia and ethnic Serbians residing in Bosnia; collectively the two groups had greater military might, and the Muslims initially avoided secession perceiving it as suicidal. The foregoing notwithstanding, the international community by 1992 had pledged to recognize the independence of Bosnia once it seceded (Annan, 2000). Resultantly, this pledge compounded by the knowledge possessed by the Muslim leaders regarding humanitarian intervention in Croatia and Iraq, gave them a sense of belief that they would be protected by the international community if they took up arms and seceded from Yugoslavia. Eventually, with the support of the ethnic Croat minority from Bosnia, the Muslims proceeded with the calls for secession. In April 1992, the Serbian forces retaliated and killed tens of thousands of fighters and civilians; the international community did not intervene decisively until 1995.

A few years later, the same scenario played itself out in the Serbian province of Kosovo (Adebajo, 2008). Independence was sought by the local ethnic Albanian majority, but they resulted to peaceful resistance throughout the 1990s due to the apparent military might of the Serbians. Despite the influx of light weaponry from Albania in 1997, most of the ethnic Albanians in Kosovo and the rebel Kosovo Liberation Army were of the firm opinion that they were no match for the heavily armored Serbian forces. Still, Woodward (2001) notes that the rebels believed that in the event they provoked the Serbians into retaliating against the Albanian population, independence would be facilitated by intervention from the international community.

Interestingly, their plan played out almost to a tee; in the late 1997, the rebels divided themselves into pockets that shot at large numbers of Serbs and the police. Subsequently, the Serbian forces retaliated in 1998 using a counter-insurgency that killed approximately 1000 Albanian civilians and rebels. A year later, NATO intervened through consistent air strikes that compelled the Serbian forces after 11 weeks to accept and withdraw from NATO occupation. Almost a decade later in 2007, this intervention led to most European states and the US recognizing the independence of Kosovo. However, Cilliers (2008) is quick to point out that the initial intervention by NATO had backfired since in March 1999, their actions compelled the Serbs to commence ethnic cleansing the saw close to 850,000 Albanians displaced and another 10,000 killed. In retaliation when the Serb forces withdrew in June 1999, the Albanians ethnically cleansed close to 100,000 and another several hundred were killed. Cilliers and Malan (2005) contends that the violence rates in Kosovo were approximately 30 times more during the NATO bombing campaign compared to the previous years of conflict before the intervention from the international community.

In support, Callaghy, Kassimir and Latham (2001a) argue that most of the deaths and displacements that took place in the Balkans were direct consequences to application of the R2P. Furthermore, Callaghy, Kassimir and Latham (2001b) believe that Muslim and Albanian militant leaders launched their challenges, which provoked retaliation from the state, premised wholly on the prospect of sympathetic foreign intervention. Thus, the unavoidable and unfortunate conclusion is that humanitarian intervention at times occasions tragedies that it intended to prevent.

2.2 The case of Darfur

The Darfur region of the northwestern Sudan (see Appendix 1 for a map of Darfur), has witnessed similar patterns as other areas across the world regarding intervention of the international community since 2003 (Collins, 2008). Between 2003 and 2004, violence was the most intense as the Janjaweed Arab Militias who were supported by the State perpetrated counter insurgency against hundreds of villages whom they suspected of harbouring and offering support to African rebels consequently converting more than 2 million Sudanese to refugees to Chad, and killing tens of thousands more (De Coning, 2005a). De Coning (2005b) notes that during this period, the international community stood by and watched and lacked courage to muster political will to facilitate military intervention. The only action that was seen from the international community was the brisk provision of aid to the millions of victims, which they could reach, of the armed conflict that was raging in the Darfur region.

It was not until August 2004, when the AU deployed close to 7,000 police and peacekeepers. Nevertheless, De Waal (2007a) asserted that despite the action from the international community, they lacked logistical support and material including fuel and air support, which could have ensured rapid reaction and reconnaissance. For several years, the peacekeepers and regional police could not protect the internally displaced camps, escort convoys of humanitarian aid, and protect the civilians in villages. According to De Waal (2007b), in 2007 the UN and the AU authorized a much bigger joint force (UNAMID) to the region comprising 20,000 troops and 26,000 personnel. Unfortunately, till early 2009, the deployment of the large force had yet to reach half the initially intimated size, and they were still waiting for the helicopters that had been requested. De Coning (2006) is of the opinion that the major powers in the world have been slow in deploying forces to the Darfur primarily to protect their interest and to avert any violent Islamic opposition against the troops already on the ground; as was the case for the troops in Afghanistan and Iraq.

Darfur is a recent example where R2P has failed. Between 1983 and 2005, Sudan has been engulfed in brutal civil war between southern rebels and the northern based regimes. Field (2004) opines that the civilians from the south bore most of the violent brunt. Commencing in 2001, in line with the emerging norm of R2P, the US broadened an international campaign to protect civilians in the south. It did this by exacting pressure on the Sudanese government to share wealth and power with the rebels. Francis et al (2005) assert that pressures from the West bore fruit in 2003 when their intervention led to Sudan agreeing to tentative peace with the south.

Unfortunately, similar to many other instances across the world, the intervention had the consequence of triggering rebellion in Darfur by militants whose objective was to copy the southern strategy of luring intervention from the international community for purposes of gaining shares of wealth and power (Flint and de Waal, 2008). Francis (2006) states that despite the brutal response from the state to rebellion in Darfur, initial responses from the international community were characterised by sanctions and condemnation. Grono (2006) adds that the initial implementation of the R2P principle only spurred on the rebels to continue fighting, with the objective of soliciting greater international intervention. The sad consequence was to increase and exacerbate the suffering of the civilians. When the Sudanese government signed a peace agreement brokered by the US in 2006, two of the three primary rebel factions vehemently refused unless they got extra concessions and more international community intervention was facilitated, as was the case in Bosnia (Grono, 2006). According to MacQueen (2002), the recalcitrance elicited further segmentation of the rebellion, anarchic violence and a breakdown in the peace process. Due to the fact that the rebels have never had opportunity of battlefield victory on their own, Kagwanja and Mutahi (2007) hypothesize that their incessant refusal to make peace is propelled by the hope of more and larger interventions from the international community under the principle of R2P. Again, this principle that was designed to reduce genocidal violence and other war related crimes has produces a contradicting effect.

2.3 The protection of Civilians and R2P

Kent and Malan (2003) point out that the UN had only addressed issues relating to humanitarian law in particular countries before the 1990's. The increased need to protect civilians was initially comprehensively dealt in the report on the situation in Africa prepared by the Secretary General that termed the protection of citizens as an important need.

Similarly, Johnstone, Tortolani and Gowan, (2005) note that this was the commencement of appreciation the protection of civilians as a separate, necessary and distinct issue in the UN. When the Canadian government incorporated the concept of protection of innocent civilians in the UNSC agendas, two fundamental Security Council resolutions (1265 and 1296) that would affect future peacekeeping missions, were released. Juma (2006) notes that the UNSC resolution 1265 was revolutionary in the sense that it expressed the desire and desire of the UNSC to address the protection of civilians in armed conflict where they were being targeted, or where their assistance is deliberately being obstructed. On the other hand, UNSC Resolution 1296 outlined the operational procedures designed to improve the UN's capacity to undertake operations meant to protect civilians.

Since 1999 Ekengard (2008) asserts that most of UN peace and non-UN peace operations were tasked with protecting innocent civilians who were being unlawfully targeted in armed conflict. Clough (n.d.) notes that the inclusion of this phrase has become standard in the language of Security Council Resolutions tasked with authorizing peace operations where the lives of innocent civilians are in peril. Subsequently, Bogland, Egnell and Lagerstrom (2008) are of the opinion that arguments have been advanced that the preservation of civilians is a major expectation in several, if not all, the peace operations. Further, Brickhill (2007) is of the opinion that the UN has been taken more concrete measures designed to ensure that they provided more and better protection; including creating a permanent police facility that would provide necessary start-up capacity for the military arm of the operations for peacekeeping. In addition, the US has come up with new strategies meant to address the robust and complex environments.

On the other hand, Curtis (2001) notes that inasmuch as there have been many institutional and thematic developments, the responses from the international community with regard to armed conflicts have been focusing on the exacerbating levels of suffering innocent civilians. Darfur is a major example with regard to the foregoing point. More so, Fasher (2012) adds that it offers an exemplar foundation to instigate the differences and overlaps between the issue of protecting civilians and the R2P due to the fact that R2P was invoked severally in Darfur particularly with regard to the calls for civilian protection. Gberie (2004) contends that Darfur was termed as a supreme humanitarian emergency, which provided a fundamental test case for R2P since the principle was endorsed at the 2005 World Summit.

The foregoing notwithstanding, Krasner (2003) emphasise that it important to appreciate the distinctions between protecting civilians and R2P; especially with respect to evaluating the attempts to protect Darfur that could be perceived as a kind of R2P response. Olsson (2010) avows that R2P was founded and embraced at the UN level, policymakers and diplomats have cautioned against interlacing agendas on protection of civilians with R2P. The reason for the same as per the opinion of Rankhumise (2006) would be tantamount to politicizing the concept of protecting civilians. Raustiala (2003) further notes that the agenda of protection is defined more broadly compared to the R2P framework. On one hand, the protection agenda encompasses the protection of the dignity and safety of individuals who are faced by imminent threats of violence, on the other hand, R2P entails the necessity to protect civilians who are confronted by mass atrocities. Still, Sudan Tribune (2013d) asserts that despite the apparent difference, there are some correlations between the two. For instance, both of them are premised on IHL and human rights, plus they are both concerned with the protection of individuals. In addition, Sudan Tribune (2013a) notes that both concepts recognize the sole responsibility of states to protect their populations. Moreover, they assert that they are not enforced as a lead up to application of military force. Sudan Tribune (2013b) agrees that this is relevant given recent debates on the necessity and usefulness to offer protection.

Further, as witnessed in the Darfur and other conflicts, civilian protection represents the core attempts to operationalise R2P (UN Refugee Agency, 2012b). However, there are major tensions that exist with regard to facilitation of protection clad as military assignments. For example, intervention from the military may lead to outcomes that are counterproductive, even in cases where there is no political will or the necessary resources to implement the same. Supportively, United Nations (2004) adds that relying on peace operations can only do so much in the formulation of adequate provisions necessary for sustainable peace. Tragically, there is no consensus regarding the activities that are enshrouded under 'protection' but also the 'how' and 'who' of protection. UN Refugee Agency (2012c) narrows this down to what or who are the real targets of protection, as well as 'who decides' and 'on what' basis? It is for this reason that there are several interpretations regarding the military concepts. SaveDarfur (n.d.) notes that NGOs, military leaders and the UN officials have a different understanding of its application.

Nonetheless, Presse (2012) is of the opinion that in order for R2P to be successfully implemented towards civilian protection, several conditions need to simultaneously takes place. They include the existence of one of the 4 mass atrocities that spur R2P, adequate and reliable capabilities to react, the readiness of the international community to risk the lives of their soldiers to go and protect non-citizens, and the unavailability of the necessary preparation and concepts to address the particular necessities of the conflict environment that are non-permissive. As this study has established so far, since its September 2005 inception, there are several strains in the R2P principle that remains unresolved to date. This needs to be considered when assessing the unavailability of answers to issues of how the international community and global leaders ought to have responded since 2003, when the Darfur armed conflict began.

CHAPTER 3 – METHODOLOGY

3.1 Research Approach

This research has employed a qualitative approach over a quantitative approach since it allows the researcher to uncover more about the experience of people, and it less expensive compared to quantitative research that demands large volumes of data that are examined using expensive measurement tools. Qualitative research addresses how things occur and why they occur (Lakshman, et al., 2007). Qualitative research is associated with text and with interpretation of meaning (Creswell, 2009). Qualitative research asked "how" and "why" which makes it the best methodology for a study of political and humanitarian intervention such as this one. Yin (2009) suggested that case studies allow an in-depth investigation of subject materials while search for an explanation of the materials that are discovered. This flexibility makes the qualitative case study an excellent choice for this study. In addition, a qualitative approach allows the researcher to analyse primary, secondary and tertiary materials related to the loss of lives in Darfur the charges in the ICC relating to al-Bashir, and the responses or lack of responses to the charges against Bashir by the UN Security Council. Secondary research relating to the issues of humanitarian intervention in Darfur and the larger issues for the legal requirement of intervention in cases that result in large-scale loss of lives has been conducted. The qualitative research is comprised of a purely textual analysis.

After identifying the objectives and aim of the research, the researcher sought to gather information pertinent to the matter at hand. Most of the material for the research was in hard copy format and the researcher had to toil endlessly in the library, rummaging several law books tracing the root causes of armed conflict, what the law provides on the same. The researcher contends that the information was too much and it was necessary to avoid going off topic. To ease into this, the researcher moved to the internet and sought to find recent commentary on the situation in Darfur, and how the concept of R2P is being abused on the basis of misconception and misunderstanding by the developed countries that form the UNSC. Similarly, the researcher was confronted by the problem of too much data and only sought data that spoke directly of the situation in Darfur with respect to R2P. Throughout the data gathering process, the researcher was guided by the "how" and "why" questions that characterise qualitative research approaches. Once the relevant information had been set aside, the researcher sought to present the same in a logical and coherent flow that would present the issues in Darfur, R2P and the role of the international community in an easy and interesting way.

3.2 Reliability and Validity

Issues of reliability and validity are a concern in any study. Reliability and validity address whether or not the data can be trusted, and whether or not the research as a whole has merit. Creswell (2011:244, 245) discussed validity at length and concluded that different types of validity are applied to various types of study. Qualitative study, He suggested that approaching the research with objectivity represents a type of validity (Creswell, 2011: 244-245, citing LeCompte and Goetz, 1982). Lincoln and Guba (1985) emphasized transferability of the conclusions as a measure of reliability (in Creswell, 2011: 244). Wolcott (1994) emphasized that the understanding of a subject that is developed is more important than a more technical form of validity (in Creswell, 2011: 245). Whittemore, Chase, and Mandle (2001, in Creswell, 2011: 245) reported that if the study is conducted with integrity, thoroughness, congruence, and sensitivity, it is likely to be valid.

Many of the needs that Creswell describes can be fulfilled by use of triangulation, or the use of multiple viewpoints to evaluate research materials (2011:251). Creswell suggested that at least two methods of triangulation be utilized in establishing validity. These methods include peer review or debriefing, in which one researcher in the group plays the role of devil's advocate in questioning the "methods, meanings, and interpretations" (Creswell, 2011:251). Another type of triangulation, referred to as negative case analysis, requires the researcher to continue refining working hypotheses or themes as the investigation continues. This is another variety of inductive research. Clarifying researcher bias as a form of triangulation (Creswell, 2011:251) can be utilized to great avail. By keeping a record of the researcher's experiences, prejudices, biases, and ideation during the investigation, the researcher can go back and determine areas of the investigation that might need to be addressed in a different light or fashion. The use of "rich, thick, description" allows the readers to participate in the evaluative process and to make their own decisions as to whether or not the researcher's conclusions are valid. In order for this to succeed, the researcher has to provide a great deal of rich detail, including that of physical descriptions and descriptions of movements and activities. Guion, Diehl, and McDonald (2011) suggest that environmental triangulation is also an important method. In environmental triangulation, key factors of accounts are compared. In addition, an effort is made to gather information relating to a variety of places, times, and seasons in order to determine if the findings would be the same when the environments is varied.

3.3 Analysis of UN documentation on R2P in the context of Darfur

UN Refugee Agency (2012a) noted that the R2P holds that state sovereignty involves the responsibility of the state to protect and the default prerogative and R2P civilians fall on the international community. In light of this, this section illuminates and reviews UN documentation on R2P in context of intervention of the case of Darfur.

3.3.1 Legal Objections to Humanitarian Intervention

The sovereignty of the state forms the basis of legal objections to humanitarian intervention; more so because of the major feature of the present international system in the division of the world into many states (UN Refugee Agency, 2012c). Presse (2012) encapsulates this to mean full independence and non-interference in internal affairs. To this end, all primary norms, practices and rules of international relations are hinged on the sovereignty and autonomy of the state. Similarly, UN Refugee Agency (2012g) adds that the traditional international relations system was based on the primary assumption that a state is the major actor in international situations.

State sovereignty has been invoked in several international documents, regional and universal, UN Refugee Agency (2012f) contends that this principle was underlined in the 1993 Montevideo Convention on the Rights and Duties of States (165 LNTS 19, article 8) that stated that 'no state has a right to intervene in the internal and external affairs of another.' Accordingly, the UN Charter declares under Article 2 (1) that it is founded on, *inter alia*, the principle of quality of its member states. In addition, Article 1 (2) emphasises the principle of self-determination and equal rights of peoples. UN Refugee Agency (2012c) explains that both concepts are corollary of the right of every state to sovereignty, independence and territorial integrity, which the non-intervention and sovereign principles aim to advance. In addition, Article 2(7) of the UN Charter articulates that there is no provision within it that would authorise intervention to matters or situations that are primarily in the jurisdiction of any state.

Therefore, opponents of humanitarian intervention perceive it as illegal and its embracing of military intervention is in contradiction of the globally acknowledged norms of non-intervention (UN Refugee Agency, 2012g). Inasmuch as there have been increments in liberal attitudes regarding intervention, the sovereignty of the states is a fundamental attribute of international law. This was exemplified by the global reaction to the forcible annexation of Kuwait by Iraq. From a legal perspective, humanitarian intervention in Darfur can be challenged on the fact that it violates Article 2(4) of the UN Charter, which insinuates total prohibition of using force in international relations, except for the exemptions mentioned in the UN Charter, which include Article 42 that denotes the use of armed force as a measure of enforcement taken by the Security Council, collective and individual self-defence as spelt out in Article 51, measures of enforcing by regional agencies under regional arrangements underlined in Article 53, authorising of peacekeeping forces by the UN General Assembly or Security Council following consent from the concerned state, and application of Article 106 that pre-empts joint action of the members of the Security Council.

In addition, UNOCHA (2013) does not conceive the chance of a legal basis for humanitarian intervention in Darfur under the UN Charter or under international law. UN Refugee Agency (2012e) suggests that any form of intervention from the international community in Darfur cannot by underpinned in international law or the UN Charter, but rather a moral choice that needs to be made by other countries.

3.3.2 Impasse in reconciling state sovereignty and humanitarian intervention

In the 54th UN General Assembly, Kofi Annan brought to the fore the impasse that is created by the unacceptability of humanitarian intervention under tenets of protecting state sovereignty at the expense of protecting innocent civilians. UN Refugee Agency (2012d) summed this dilemma as the competing normative values in international law; what is more important between maintaining relations between states and protecting the fundamental rights of citizens. Raustiala (2003) resigns to the fact that sovereignty versus humanity is not only intricate and fraught with contradictions that cannot be easily solved.

On one hand, intervention of the international community in Darfur would be tantamount to infringing Article 2 (4) of the UN Charter and this might lead to dire implications for international security and peace, which may be triggered by international intervention that lacks a backing or a mandate from the UN, then the members of the UN Security Council distance themselves from the actions, the result could be further acts of war in the intervening countries from the armed rebels or perpetrators of war in this other country (UN Refugee Agency, 2012b). On the other hand, it is paramount to uphold the concepts of humanity. Rankhumise (2006) argues that respecting human rights is necessary for the sustenance of international peace.

The logic of protecting human rights stems from the fact that failure of intervention from the international community in Darfur violates the Genocide Convention, and encourages repressive regimes to continue perpetrating evils on people since they will go unpunished. This means that international orders that tolerate any of the 4 mass atrocities that trigger the R2P is unstable since both international and national orders are closely intertwined and both derive their stability and legitimacy from their ability to protect innocent civilians during armed conflict or against any other form of violence. To this end, this impasse has been dealt with under international law by placing premiums on the provisions that protect human rights or develop and ensure peace on the international scene. Olsson (2010) asserts that this stance has eroded the principle of state sovereignty.

3.3.3 Tackling the legal objections

Krasner (2003) is of the opinion that developments over the last five decades have seen the original ideology of sovereignty change. The legal interpretation of sovereignty underscored in Article 2(7) of the UN Charter has been changing gradually since 1945. There are five reasons that have led to this change underlined in the *Early Warning, Assessment and the Responsibility to Protect* (A/64/864), The *Responsibility to Protect: Timely and Decisive Response* (A/66/874-S/2012/578). First, sovereignty has suffered from the internationalisation of human rights, which has seen the removal of human rights from the domain of individual sovereign states to the international community. Second, the increase of global interconnection and interdependence characterised by globalisation has favoured the unifying of legal, economic, environmental and political issues. Third, Gberie (2004) agrees that the technological advancements in telecommunications have also been linked to human rights issues, have played a part in the erosion of state sovereignty. Resultantly, the control exercised by governments over the availability and spreading of information has been eroded. Fourth, the increment in participation by international organisations, individuals, non-governmental organisations and other non-state actors illustrates that respect for state sovereignty has shifted. Finally, the changing patterns of armed conflict, the intervention from the international community has led to the demise of the Cold War and the erosion of the principle of state sovereignty.

3.4 Roles and limitations of the International Criminal Court in internal conflict

Enforcing both human rights law and international humanitarian law is still a major challenge despite the coming into force of the Rome Statute and functioning of the ICC since 1st July 2002, which was designed to bring justice to individuals who perpetrate war crimes, torture, crimes against humanity, and genocide. Currently, 120 countries are party to the ICC, out of which 33 are African (Brickhill, 2007). The ICC can prosecute individuals who have allegedly breached the provisions of IHL, and its jurisdiction extends to the aforementioned crimes regardless of where and when they were carried out. In addition, the ICC prosecutor can commence investigations based on referrals from a state party to the Rome Statute. According to Curtis (2001), the ICC identifies the pertinence of domestic criminal jurisdiction before it commences any case against a country. States have a duty to conduct investigations and prosecute offenders, regardless of their position in government, when they are found to be guilty.

Ekengard (2008) notes that the Sudanese government has set up its own special courts for the crimes committed in Darfur in order to prevent the ICC from exercising jurisdiction in the country. Still, the efforts of the governments to set up a robust judiciary system have received criticisms as insufficient. Juma (2006) asserts that the UN Security Council passed Resolution 1593 informed by the provision of Article 13(b) of the Rome Statute against Sudan requesting the ICC to conduct investigate war crimes that were committed by the Sudanese government and other parties responsible for the conflict in Darfur. However, Sudan is not a party to the Rome Statute and it would be unjust and illegal for the ICC to intervene and carry out investigations (Johnstone, Tortolani and Gowan, 2005). However, the ICC contends that the UN Security Council Resolution is binding on all UN member states, such as Sudan, regardless of the fact that it has not ratified the Rome Statute. ICC has issued arrest warrants against its president Al-Bashir for genocide, rape, war crimes, ethnic cleansing and crimes against humanity.

Further, it has issued summons to appear for the rebel leaders to answer to charges of war crimes, as is illustrated in the Table 3.1 below

Case	Status
Former Interior Minister Ahmad Muhammad Harun and alleged former militia leader Ali Kushayb	Arrest warrants issued in May 2007. Suspects at large. Harun is governor of Sudan's Southern Kordofan state.
Darfur rebel leader Bahar Idriss Abu Garda	Prosecutor's case dismissed by ICC judges in February 2010.
Darfur rebel leaders Abdallah Banda Abakaer Nourain, and Saleh Mohammed Jerbo Jamus	Pre-trial phase; charges confirmed in March 2011. Banda and Jerbo appeared voluntarily before the Court in response to summonses in June 2010.
Sudanese President Omar Hassan al Bashir	Arrest warrant issued in March 2009 for war crimes and crimes against humanity and Additional arrest warrant issued for genocide in July 2010.
Former Chief of Staff of SLA-Unity and currently integrated into Justice and Equality Movement Saleh Mohammed Jerbo Jamus	On the basis of his individual criminal responsibility under article 25(3)(a)
Current Minister of National Defence and former Minister of the Interior and former Sudanese President's Special Representative in Darfur Abdel Raheem Muhammad Hussein	Arrest warrant issued in March 2012 for Crimes against humanity and War crimes on the basis of his individual criminal responsibility under article 25(3)(a)

Table 3.1: Rebel leaders in the Sudan and the charges against them

Many African leaders have criticized the actions of the ICC basing their arguments on the fact that all the active cases before it are all from Africa (Kent and Malan, 2003). MacQueen (2002) contends that the ICC can rightfully be accused of targeting African countries owing to this fact; besides, there are many other atrocities that have been committed to other parts of the World. Attempts of the ICC prosecutor to arrest a sitting African head of state, Omar Hassan Al Bashir, has been a topic of debate by many African leaders. Subsequently, Grono (2006) asserts that the AU has refused to cooperate with the ICC's request to arrest the president. Chad, Mali and Kenya all of which are parties to the ICC and they have all failed to arrest Al-Bashir on his visit to the countries. Despite supporting the significance of the ICC, the AU criticizes it on grounds of remaining silent for mass atrocities committed in Argentina, Myanmar and Iraq. They collectively labeled the ICC as having discriminatory practices and double standards.

Despite the foregoing, Francis (2006) argues that ICC could not have commenced its work were it not for Africa acknowledging its jurisdiction. Therefore, the arguments presented by the AU are unjustifiable and unreasonable especially when it comes to the reality of genocide, torture, war crimes and crimes against humanity that have been committed merely because other perpetrators from other regions are yet to be targeted. If anything, Flint and de Waal (2008) argue that the responsibility of the cooperation in bringing justice to perpetrators of the

Darfur conflicts depends on them, to ensure effective workings of the ICC compared to other regions. More so, the AU could be said to have stood by and watched as gross abuses of human rights were being facilitated in Darfur.

In addition, the AU was of the opinion that Al Bashir should be protected and immune pursuant to the provisions of Article 98(1) of the Rome Statute that notes that the ICC cannot proceed with any requests for assistance or surrender that would require the State to act contrary to its sovereign obligations with regard to the diplomatic immunity of property or person of a third state. The only situation that ICC can facilitate such arrest is when cooperation of the third state is obtained; this will act as a waiver of the immunity. Nonetheless, Francis et al (2005) argues that Article 27(2) of the Rome Statute contradicts with the previous provision by asserting that special procedural rules or immunities attached to the capacity of a person regardless of whether it is under international or national law, shall not curtail the ICC from exercising its jurisdiction over such an individual.

CHAPTER 4 – THE NEED TO CHANGE THE ROLE OF THE INTERNATIONAL COMMUNITY IN DARFUR

4.1 Failure of R2P in Darfur

The HW and ICG and the Aegis Trust invoked the Principle of the R2P framework to demand for effective international action over Darfur (Field, 2004). De Coning (2006) understands these calls as euphemisms for military intervention since the international community failed in exerting force on the Sudanese government to neutralize the *Janjaweed* or front their troops to participate in intervening in Darfur. De Waal (2007c) argues that NATO ought to have already sent troops to quell the conflict in Darfur. However, De Waal (2007b) warns against the evaluation that the international community's commitment to R2P failed because international forces were not deployed to Darfur as quickly as many would deem possible. This means that military intervention ought not to have been perceived as core in establishing R2P in the region.

De Waal (2007a) further notes that the R2P is shrouded in many unresolved tensions. For instance the 2005 World Summit Outcome Document is seen to be deliberately vague on the moments at which sovereign responsibilities should devolve onto international actors. In particular Paragraph 139 on the resources and mechanisms needed to react to real cases ignores the potential responses that are unique from the use of force that could have been implemented. Furthermore, De Coning (2005b) argues that R2P is all about selectivity since it was not designed to handle all imaginable cases that could happen anywhere in the world. In addition, advocacy for R2P has converted protection of civilians to an intervention issue instead of supporting a political process. According to De Coning (2005a) since there was no workable political process, designing R2P under the semblance of a major UN force underscored in Chapter VII was unfeasible in the respect for Darfur. Collins (2008), notes that a danger of such advocacy lies in the fact that it will overlook major questions concerning the intervention levels that can be accomplished. Callaghy, Kassimir and Latham (2001b) argue that military civilian protection in ongoing conflicts should never act as a replacement for the responsibilities of the government. Instead it should be perceived as a means of reinforcing them. In addition, proponents of intervention of NATO in Darfur do not fully explain the difference that the intervention would realise. Interventions by the military such as those in Iraq and Afghanistan illustrate the extents of what robust military presence and power can accomplish on the ground. Second, Callaghy, Kassimir and Latham (2001a) note that it is important not to underestimate the intricacies that ail Darfur in terms of political disagreements. Given the size of Sudan and the roots of the crisis, and the means by which intervention from the international community means that the prospects of successful outcomes on the back of military actions is questionable. In the event that Sudan had not consented to the unilateral intervention, there would have been aggressive resistance that would have led to reduced protection of large populations and minimized access of humanitarian agencies. As pointed out by Cilliers (2008) lack of adequate strategies and political support to bear the human and financial costs would have led to neglecting the global duty to protect civilians.

The expectations to what peacekeeping operations could achieve in the Darfur conflict were set too high, more so in light of their ambiguous mandates and the inadequacy of proper resources and troops. In addition, R2P has not yet generated enough political will to protect civilians in Darfur (Cilliers and Malan, 2005). Though failure of the international intervention to intervene in timely fashion in Darfur as underpinned by the R2P is punctuated by several challenges in line with implementing them, the assessment of the R2P should not be compounded to the effectiveness of deployment and response of the military. According to Woodward (2001) appraisal to the most pronounced responses to Darfur, UNAMID and AMIS indicates an absence of timely and unified prioritization of coercive legal, economic, political and diplomatic actions nearing military reaction. However, Adebajo (2008) argues that such measures could have been implemented on the notion of facilitating protection. Nonetheless, the challenges that faced the implementation of R2P in the Darfur should not be adjudged as its overall failure. Still, there is need to change the present state of affairs with regard to ensuring that innocent civilians are actually protected from armed conflict.

4.2 Selective State practice

4.2.1 Interest-Based Selectivity

The interests of the international community have to a large extent affected their involvement towards the Darfur Crisis (Annan, 2000). Bellamy, Williams and Griffin (2004) argue that the role of the US during the Darfur Crisis is interestingly similar as it is different from its reaction to the Rwandan genocide. The US government was extremely forthright in condemning the atrocities perpetuated in Darfur; it also openly spoke against the role of the Sudanese government in assisting the Janjaweed militia in carrying out the war crimes (Bach, 2008).

However, the case for the Rwandan genocide was treated differently by the Clinton Administration and US officials around the world did not describe the situation as 'genocide', yet its outspoken nature towards the harrowing crimes taking place in Sudan seemed to be an indirect mockery of the genocide situation. In line with this, Appiah-Mensah (2006) notes that the US was reluctant to offering financial aid and logistical support to the OAU peacekeeping forces.

An important aspect to consider according to Aboagye (2007) is that the involvement of the US in Africa ought to be appraised through alteration of its strategic interests after 9/11. Before attacks on 2 US embassies in East Africa, the US did not have strategic interests in Africa, but it was forced to conduct retaliatory attacks against pharmaceutical factory in Khartoum. Its attack on Sudan was strategic and Natarajan (2011) terms it as a turning point for the US with regard to policies in Africa, even after placing Sudan on its wanted list for habouring terrorism in the 1990s, the US changed it tact and termed it as a country that was cooperating with its war on terror; while at the same time, the events at Darfur were unfolding. Mehta (2009) contends that issues of arms control, oil, maritime security, and fighting terrorism are all aspects that have become important to the US after 9/11, and all of a sudden Sudan was willing to cooperate on these aspects. This means that from the part of the government, there was no need to attack to attack the Sudanese government despite being involved in the gruesome acts in the Darfur region. Interestingly, the US changed its stance over the actions in Darfur following a change of national interests.

As well, the Chinese became actively involved in the brokering peace deals in the Darfur region after oil was discovered in 2005. Both the US and China were reluctant to send their troops as their interests would be scampered, instead both countries condemned the acts and demanded that Janjaweed militia and Sudanese officials be brought to justice via an international tribunal similar to that of Rwanda and Yugoslavia. Jennings and Watts (1994) affirm that international intervention in protecting civilians should not be averted because of protection of self interests, it is more important to protect human lives.

4.2.2 Racial-based selectivity

According to Jackson (2002), the international community has been shifting action meant to help Darfur and understating as another African problem that has a tendency of emerging now and then. Bolton (2005) points out that Africans are perceived as less and different from other human beings and it does not make sense to spend so much money in intervening on their behalf. The nature of inaction and the vague calls for the formation of international tribunals supports a racial-based selectivity approach on the part of the international community. Save Darfur (n.d.) adds that the delay in assisting civilians caught up in armed conflict in Africa is because the interveners see them as all black and they are used to these kinds of conflict. Supportively, Aboagye (2007) states that the fact there are Arabs and Muslims involved in killing one another in Darfur has facilitated delays in intervention from the international community since most of the terrorist attacks that take place in other countries are perpetrated by terrorist camps that are largely comprised of Arab and Muslim extremist groups. Therefore, there is a blanket application of attitude towards all Arabs and Muslims in the Darfur region, Appiah-Mensah (2006) does not call this by any other name other than racism, a scourge that will only lead to the deaths of more tens of thousands innocent civilians.

Bach (2008) gives the example of the quick humanitarian intervention in Kosovo, which is inhibited by Europeans, and the aid effort in this region is more generous compared to the ones that feed Darfur or the Congo, which is more than 200 times larger than Kosovo. Therefore, Africans are not deemed to be worth the investment since they are different in life and in shape. Bellamy, Williams and Griffin (2004) add that such perceptions actually shape the national interests. The reason for this is that when one looks at another person more differently, other rationalizations that are more politically correct take centre stage. In order for international intervention in implementing the principle of R2P to successfully work, Adebajo (2008) argues that it is necessary to take away the misconception of other people as being different; the foregoing needs to change if more lives are to be saved.

4.3 Inadequate Humanitarian Discourse

Woodward (2001) believes that humanitarian intervention has failed in Darfur because of the persistence of scanty humanitarian discourse ever since the Rwandan genocide. Cilliers (2008) contends that failure on the part of international intervention in Rwanda was the lack or inability to ascertain the atrocities on the Tutsi was made up of the genocide. The reason for the lack of foresight was the belief that once, an event is declared as genocide, it will automatically invoke the 1948 UN Convention on the Prevention and Punishment of the Crime of Genocide, and this would necessitate international action.

However, in the case of the Sudan many world leaders did not shy away from coming out and openly condemning the genocidal violence that was taking place in the Darfur region, and its perpetrators were no other than the Janjaweed militia who were being supported by the Sudanese government. Nonetheless, Cilliers and Malan (2005) argue that the fact that other leaders failed in terming the atrocity as genocide instead opting for other R2P wars could have been the cause of the international community's slothful reaction to the crisis. Consequently, despite having good definitions, Callaghy, Kassimir and Latham (2001a) notes that the lack of proper implementation of the Genocide Convention has converted it to a mere document that only holds much promise with no prospect of being applied. In addition, Callaghy, Kassimir and Latham (2001b) further notes that the term genocide is often used by international officials and statesmen on a selective basis. Besides, The Report of the International Commission termed the events of Rwanda as crimes against humanity, conspicuously failing to incorporate the fact that the attacks focused on exterminating an entire group of people. Therefore, the lack of terming the effects of conflict as they actually are has taken the centre stage and has eventually become politicized and this has left little room for impartial humanitarian action.

Still, another failure on the part of international intervention was the fact that there has been minimal media coverage on the area, which could have exposed the situations as they actually are on the ground (Collins, 2008). De Coning (2006) believes that in so doing, perhaps international intervention would have come much faster. However, the media only gained interest in the region every time an issue they thought interesting came to the fore, and was worth writing about, and not daily reporting of the atrocities taking place.

4.4 Review of documentary evidence regarding the process of intervention

According to Sudan Tribune (2013a), UNAMID replaced an underequipped and underfunded AU peacekeeping mission in Darfur in 2008. Unfortunately, UNAMID remains without the requisite equipment to protect the more than 2.7 IDPs residing in camps across Darfur, and another 300,000 in Chad. The UN projects that there are about 4.7 million Sudanese people in Darfur, from a total population of 6 million that are affected by the conflict. The Sudanese government has inhibited the deployment of peacekeeping forces, refused to prosecute any persons responsible for the commission of atrocities in Darfur, avoided any negotiations with the rebel groups, and expelled 13 international humanitarian aid groups from Darfur.

Sudan Tribune (2013b) agrees with humanitarian sources that most of the unrest being witnessed in Darfur is affiliated to Arab groups that are supporting the Al-Bashir led government, which fight among themselves, the regime, commit most of the rapes, shootings and other forms of violence against humanitarian aid groups that have been sent to assist the innocent civilians residing in the displaced camps. Moreover, there are many armed agencies that are operating in many of Darfur's towns; this makes it difficult to know who is in charge of security.

The SRF rebels, including SLM, JEM led by Abdel Wahid Al-Nur, SPLM-N and SLM-MM called for international intervention in ensuring that there is holistic peace process that will facilitate elections that will see the end of the current regime (Sudan Tribune, 2013c). Nonetheless, the AU is involved in the mediation of the conflicting Darfur regions, South Kordofan and Blue Nile states is vehemently denying to listen to their requests; the AU is urging all rebel leaders to come to the negotiating table without any preconditions. Consequently, the rebel leaders are accusing the AU of being under the beck and call of the Sudanese government; hence, they are refusing to comply to their requests since the AU believes that the only way to communicate is through a mediator yet it only listens to the one party in the conflict; the Sudanese government. The Sudan Tribune (2013a) notes that the constant bickering and back and forth situations between the conflicting parties will only lead to the commission of more atrocities, since the international community is involved and appears to be partisan.

Laessing (2013) contends that the international community is facing a hard time in Darfur due to the gold rush. The current government has been complacent and allows one militia group to control the gold mines. However, the international peace efforts are still pushing to have the warring rebel groups into a Qatar-sponsored deal that Khartoum signed in 2011. Prendergast and Ismail (2013) stated that the international community on the ground in Darfur are contradicting reports from journalists and diplomats that the civil war is nearing an end. In addition, he points out that peace efforts since the mid-2000s in Darfur have exacerbated conflict, instead of reducing it.

Most peace deals have concentrated on individual rebel commanders who end up becoming militia leaders sponsored by the government. He further adds that there has been no proposal from any peacekeeping force that has tackled the core issues that have propelled conflict in Darfur, they are perceived to advance their own selfish interests; consequently, they have all been rejected by the rebel groups and the greater Darfur population. In addition, international interventions in Darfur have been far from implementing peace efforts in other areas of the Sudan that are engulfed in war. Therefore, the support from the UN, the US and other diplomats for this divided strategy supports Khartoum's divide and conquer plan and subsequently reduce any chances for sustainable peace in Sudan. Prendergast and Ismail (2013) further note that the answer to ensure long lasting peace in Darfur is to comprehensively address the primary causation factors of the conflicts by the international community.

The situation in Darfur is explosive at best. On 13 July 2013, Seven UNAMID military peacekeepers were murdered in an ambush, and 17 military and police personnel were wounded (UNAMID, 2013). Exactly one month later, the East Darfur governor survived an assassination attempt after being attacked in worsening tribal tensions (Sudan Tribune, 2013a). In the intervening month, seventy human rights experts and experts on the Sudan petitioned the UN Security Council to consider intervention based on continued and escalating acts of violence against civilians, the need for humanitarian aid, and the need to hold responsibility for serious human rights violations (Sudan Tribune, 2013b). The response to this request seems to have been worsening hostilities. It is for this reason that no specific list of current documents is provided.

CHAPTER 5 – CONCLUSION AND RECOMMENDATION

5.1 Conclusion

Following the Rwandan genocide, debate became rife on whether there are any pointers on when and how the international community can intervene to put an end to the internal conflicts and widespread abuses of human rights. 10 years after the Rwandan Genocide and several meetings of seeking a way forward, the response from the international community to the armed clashes in Darfur, which commenced in 2003, seem to be a case of history repeating itself.

De Coning, (2005a) contends that the international community has failed Darfur, Rwanda and other countries stifled in armed conflict resulting in the deaths and displacement of millions of civilians. The argument over responsibility to protect and respect of a nation's sovereignty has been in the limelight as far as Darfur is concerned. The question lingers on whether the UN should protect people's human rights or passively observe, without having to actively protect the people. Although the case of Darfur is not yet concluded, much of the story appeared to have already unfolded. What can so far be concluded is the fact that political leaders of the world have not learnt from Rwanda's genocide. After the genocide happened, political leaders swore never again to allow wars that would come near becoming genocidal. Rwanda's genocide had many lessons for the leaders across the globe and the UN. After Rwanda experienced genocide, the term "never again" appears to have been the quote of those days. However, Darfur's case makes one think that there is a need for global leaders to go beyond "never again." It appears that what lacks in many nations is the lack of political will. If there is political will on the part of leaders, there will definitely be some form of commitment to implement what is contained in the very nicely worded documents and peace agreements in Sudan. Nevertheless, it appears that the idea of human rights has not been treated as urgent. This probably explains why another genocide had to be committed in Darfur so that the UN could expressly come out with "responsibility to protect" principles. Contrastingly, even after the UN initiated the R2P, people in Darfur have continued to suffer human rights violations.

5.2 Recommendations

Following the foregoing discovery in this research, the following recommendations have been informed and suggested by the prevailing state of affairs whereby the law of protecting innocent civilians is already in place, but implementing it is slow, there is an element of lack of political will, and other unjust albeit underlying reasons for the inaction from the international community to assist innocent Africans who are caught up in armed conflict. This research puts the following recommendations

- The authorization of peacekeeping forces ought to be clearly worded to avoid ambiguity that will reduce the likelihood of different interpretations, such as imminent threat and rules of engagement. Different interpretations occur within peacekeeping forces on the premise of country of origin and rank, as well as on the part of the UN Department of Peacekeeping Operations.

- The UN should come up with a comprehensive doctrine that is fully operational for purposes of protecting innocent civilians during armed conflict. The mandates or authorization for peacekeepers that are operating in armed conflict situations ought to incorporate tenets of human rights law, IHL, and the Principle of R2P.

- Race-based and interest based selectivity should be abolished on the part of the able and willing countries, such as China and the US, whose interests seem to be pegged on oil, arms control and fighting terrorism and not on protecting the lives of civilians. This will see quicker facilitation of deployment of troops in the armed conflict regions such as Darfur.

- Further training needs to be facilitated in improving the preparation of human rights officers to include IHL, human rights law, and requisite national laws. This will be essential in removing bias on the reports regarding the ineffectiveness of R2P and rapid deployment of the military in these sections. Moreover, it will be beneficial in telling the real story and the caution preceding inaction on the part of the international community towards conflict marred areas.

- The current laws that prohibit the violation of human rights and IHL ought to be buttressed in order to ensure proper application during implementation. In addition, there should be new laws to enforce applications that are facilitated by the UN Security Resolutions and the Rome Statute; these laws should be reflected on the actual mandates, which is what the commanders in units of peacekeeping respond to. Further, the UN should strengthen the application and reliance of legal institutions in the conduction, monitoring of investigations in areas such as Darfur that are marred by armed conflict.

Appendix

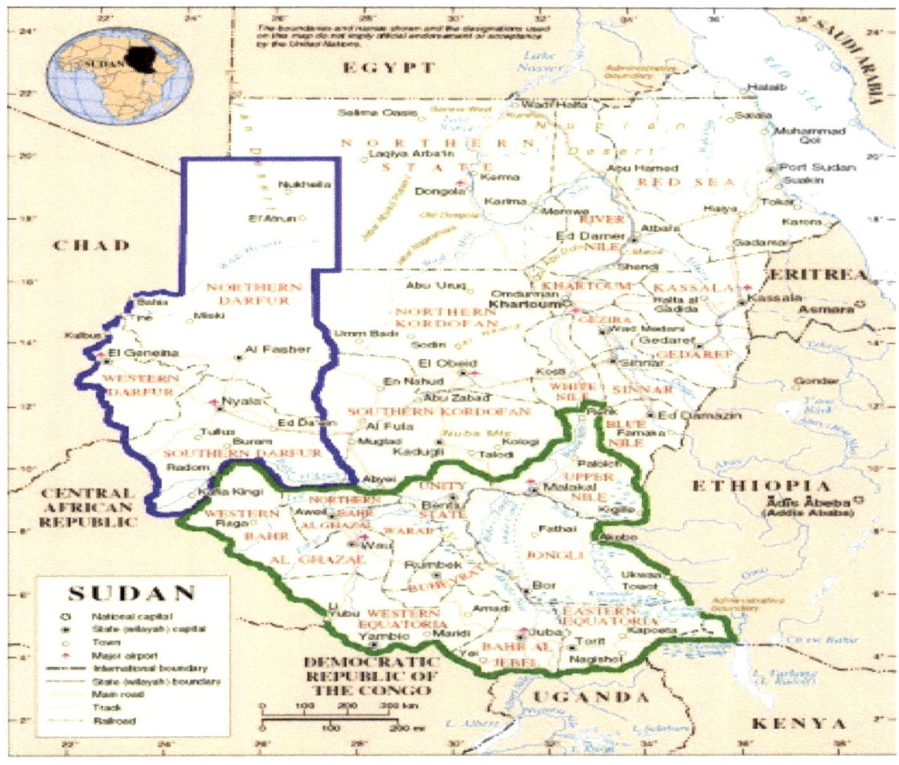

Source: http:www.tomokriznar.com/slike/zemljevidi-sudan/juzni-sudan_darfur.jpg

Bibliography

Aboagye, F. 2007. *The Hybrid Operation for Darfur: a Critical Review of the Mechanism.* ISS Paper 149.

Adebajo, A. 2008. *The Peacekeeping Travails of the AU and the Regional Economic Communities. In The African Union and its Institutions,* Akokpari, J., NdingaMuvumba, A. and Murithi, T. (eds.). Johannesburg: Fanele.

Annan, K. 2000. We the Peoples: the Role of the United Nations in the 21st Century. *UN Millenium Report.* New York: United NationsDepartment of Public Information.

Appiah-Mensah, S. 2006. The African Union Mission in Sudan: Darfur Dilemmas. *African Security Review,* 15(1): 2 – 19.

Bach, D. 2008. The AU and the EU. In *The African Union and its Institutions,* Akokpari, J., Ndinga-Muvumba, A. and Murithi, T. (eds.). Johannesburg: Fanele.

Bellamy, A.J., Williams, P. and Griffin. 2004. *Understanding Peacekeeping.* Cambridge: Polity Press.

Bolton, J. 2005. Letter to the UN Security Council, August 30, 2005, regarding the Draft Outcome document for Responsibility to Protect. Available at http://www.responsibilitytoprotect.org/files/US_Boltonletter_R2P_30Aug05[1].pdf.

Callaghy, T.M. Kassimir, R. and Latham, R. (eds.). 2001b. *Intervention and Transnationalism in Africa: Global-Local Networks of Power.* Cambridge: Cambridge University Press.

Callaghy, T.M. Kassimir, R. and Latham, R.2001a. Introduction: Transboundary Formations, Intervention, Order and Authority. In *Intervention and Transnationalism in Africa: Global-Local Networks of Power,* Callaghy, T.M., Kassimir, R. and Latham, R. (eds.). Cambridge: Cambridge University Press.

Cilliers, J. and Malan, M. 2005. *Progress With the African Standby Force.* ISS Paper98.

Cilliers, J. 2008. *The African Standby Force: An Update on Progress.* ISS Paper160.

Collins, R.O. 2008. *A History of Modern Sudan.* Cambridge: Cambridge University Press.

Crabtree B, Miller W, eds. 1999. *Doing Qualitative Research*. 2nd ed. Newbury Park, Calif: Sage.

Creswell, J., 2009. *Research Design: Qualitative, Quantitative, and Mixed Methods Approaches*. 3rd ed. Thousand Oaks: Sage.

Creswell, J., 2011. *Qualitative Inquiry and Research Design: Chooing Among Five Approaches*. Thousand Oaks: Sage.

De Coning, C. 2005a. A Peacekeeping Stand-by System for SADC: Implementing the African Stand-by Force Framework in Southern Africa. In *People, States and Regions: Building a Collaborative Security Regime in Southern Africa*, Hammerstad, A. (ed.). Bramfontein: South African Institute of International Affairs.

De Coning, C. 2005b. The Civilian Dimensions of the African Standby Force System. *Conflict Trends,* (4): 10 – 16.

De Coning, C. 2006. The Future of Peacekeeping in Africa. In *Peacekeeping – Peacebuilding: Preparing for the Future*, Ojanen, H. (ed.). Helsinki: Finnish Institute of International Affairs.

De Waal, A. (ed.). 2007b. *War in Darfur and the Search for Peace*. Harvard: Global Equity Initiative.

De Waal, A. 2007a. *Sudan: the Turbulent State. In War in Darfur and the Search for Peace,* De Waal, A. (ed.). Harvard: Global Equity Initiative.

De Waal, A. 2007c. *Darfur's Elusive Peace. In War in Darfur and the Search for Peace*, De Waal, A. (ed.). Harvard: Global Equity Initiative.

Field, S. (ed.). 2004. *Peace in Africa: Towards a Collaborative Security Regime*. Johannesburg: Institute for Global Dialogue.

Flint, J. and de Waal, A. 2008. *Darfur: a New History of a Long War*. New York: Zed Books.

Francis, D.J. 2006. *Uniting Africa*. Aldershot: Ashgate Publishing.

Francis, D.J. Faal, M., Kabia, J. and Ramsbotham, A. 2005. *Dangers of CoDeployment: UN Co-Operative Peacekeeping in Africa*. Aldershot: Ashgate Publishing

Grono, N. 2006. Briefing – Darfur: the International Community's Failure to Protect. *African Affairs*, 105(421): 621 – 631.

Guion, L. A., Diehl, D. C., and McDonald, D. 2011. *Triangulation: Establishing the Validity of Qualitative Studies*. Department of Family, Youth and Community Sciences, Florida Cooperative Extension Service, Institute of Food and Agricultural Sciences, University of Florida.

Jackson, J., 2002. Sovereignty, Subsidiarity, and Separation of Powers: The High-wire Balancing Act of Globalization. In: D. S. J. Kennedy, ed. *The Political Economy of International Trade Law: Essays in Honour of Robert E. Hudec*. Cambridge, MA: Cambridge University Press.

Jennings, R. and Watts, A., 1992. *Oppenheim's International Law, Volume 1*. 9th ed. London: Longman.

Johnstone, I. Tortolani, B.C. and Gowan, R. 2005. The Evolution of UN Peacekeeping: Unfinished Business. *Die Friedens-Warte Journal of International Peace and Organization*, 3 – 4: 55 – 72.

Juma, M.K. (ed.). 2006. *Compendium of Key Documents Relating to Peace and Security in Africa*. Pretoria: Pretoria University Law Press.

Kagwanja, P. and Mutahi, P. 2007. *Protection of Civilians in African Peace Missions: The Case of the African Union Mission in Sudan, Darfur*. ISS Paper 139.

Kent, V. and Malan, M. 2003. The African Standby Force: Progress and Prospects. *African Security Review*, 12(3):71 – 81.

King, G. K. R. and. V. S., 1994. *Designing Social Inquiry: Scientific Inference in Qualitative Inquiry*. Princeton, NY: Princeton University Press.

Lakshman, M. et al., 2007. Symposium: Clinical Epidemiology and Research Methods II: Quantitative vs. Qualitative Research Methods.. *Indian Journal of Pediatrics,* 67(5), pp. 369-377.

MacQueen, N. 2002. *United Nations Peacekeeping in Africa since 1960.* Great Britain: Pearson Education.

Mehta, V., 2009. *The UN Doctrine on the Responsibility to Protect: Can it be Enforced to Prevent Wars, Genocides and Crims Aainst Humanity.* Kendal, South Lakeland and Lancaster City United Nations Association.

Natarajan, M. ed, 2011. *International Crime and Justice..* Cambridge : Cambridge University.

Stainback, S. and. S. W., 1988. *Understanding and Conducting Wualitative Research.* Reston, VA: Council for Exceptional Children.

Woodward, S., 2001. *Humanitarian War.* London, ODI, POLIS at University of Leeds and CAFOD, London, p. 24.

Secondary Sources

Associated Press, 2012. *4 Peacekeepers Killed in Darfur Shooting United Nations Says.* [Online] Available at: http://www.foxnews.com/world/2012/12/21/4-peacekeepers-killed-in-darfur-shooting-united-nations-says/ [Accessed 21 December 2012].

BBC News. 2013. Sudan Profile. *BBC News Africa.* [Online] Available at: http://www.bbc.co.uk/news/world-africa-14094995 [Accessed 12 December 2013]

Bogland, K. Egnell, R. and Lagerstrom, M. 2008. *The African Union – A Study Focusing on Conflict Management.* [Online]. Available at: http://www.foa.se./upload/projects/Africa/foir2475.pdf. [Accessed 12 December 2013].

Brickhill, J., 2007. Protecting Civilians Through Peace Agreements: Challenges and Lessons of the Darfur Peace Agreement. *Institute for Security Studies #138,* May, pp. 1-16.

Clough, M. n.d. Darfur: Whose Responsibilityto Protect? *Human Rights Watch.* [Online]. Available at: http://www.responsibilitytoprotect.org/index.php?module=uploadsandfunc=downloadandfileId=42. [Accessed 12 December 2013].

Curry, L. A., Nembhard, I. M., and Bradley, E. H. , 2009. Qualitative and mixed methods provide unique contributions to outcomes research. *Circulation*,*119*(10), 1442-1452.

Curtis, D., 2001. *Politics and Humanitarian Aid: Debates, Dilemmas and Dissention..* London, ODI: POLIS at University of Leeds and CAFOD.

Ekengard, A. 2008. *The African Union Mission in Sudan (AMIS): Experiences and*

Fasher, E., 2012. *UNAMID: Alleged Air Strikes Cause Displacement N Darfur.* [Online] Available at: http://www.radiodabanga.org/node/40039 [Accessed 21 December 2012].

Gberie, L., 2004. The Darfur Crisis: A Test Case for Humanitarian Intervention. *KAIPTC Papers #1*, September, pp. 1-11.

Kagwanja, P. and. M. P., 2007. Protectio of Civilians in African Peace Missions: The Case of the African Union Mission in Sudan, Darfur, Paper 139. *Institute for Security Studie*, pp. 1-20.

Krasner, S. D., 2003. *Sovereignty: A Conversation with Steven D. Krasner* [Interview] (31 March 2003).

Kushkush, I. 2013. New Strife in Darfur leaves many seeking refuge. *The New York Times* [Online] Available at: http://www.nytimes.com/2013/05/24/world/africa/new-strife-in-darfur-leaves-many-seeking-refuge.html?ref=sudanand_r=0 [Accessed 12 December 2013]

Laessing, U. 2013. Gold Rush Fueling Darfur Conflict. *The Globe and Mail.* [Online] Available at: http://www.theglobeandmail.com/news/world/gold-rush-fuelling-darfur-conflict/article14740230/?page=all [Accessed 12 December 2013].

Lessons Learned. [Online]. Available at: http://www.foi.se/upload/projects/Africa/foir2559.pdf. [Accessed 12 December 2013].

Olsson, O., 2010. After Janjaweed? Socioeconomic IMpacts of the Conflict in Darfur. *Working Papers in Economics #429*, January, pp. 1-32.

Prendergast, J. and Ismail, O. 2013. Darfur's still burning. *The Daily Beast.* [Online] Available at: http://www.thedailybeast.com/articles/2013/06/13/darfur-s-still-burning.html [Accessed 12 December 2013].

Presse, A.F. 2012. Curfew in Sudan's troubled Darfur: media. *Capital News* [Online] Available at: http://www.capitalfm.co.ke/news/2012/09/curfew-in-sudans-troubled-darfur-media/ [Accessed 12 December 2013].

Radio Dabinga, 2012. *Saraf Omra Hospital Overloaded as 'New' Disease Emerges.* [Online] Available at: http://www.radiodabanga.org/node/40037 [Accessed 21 December 2012].

Rankhumise, P., 2006. Civilian (In)security in the Darfur Region of Sudan. *Institute for Security Studies*, March, pp. 1-20.

Raustiala, K., 2003. Rethinking the Sovereignty Debate in International Economy. *Journal of International Economic Law,* 6(4), pp. 841-878.

SaveDarfur n.d. *What has happened in Darfur?* [Online] Available at: http://www.savedarfur.org/pages/primer [Accessed 12 December 2013].

Sudan Tribune, 2013a. East Darfur governor survives assassination attempt as tribal tensions worsen. Sudan Tribune, 13 August 2013. Available from http://www.sudantribune.com/spip.php?article47636

Sudan Tribune, 2013b. UNSC must address Sudan's worsening crises with a more effective approach. Sudan Tribune, 24 July 2013. Available from http://www.sudantribune.com/spip.php?article47383

Sudan Tribune. 2013. Humanitaran cessation of hostilities should not be limited to Darfur: JEM. *The Sudan Tribune*[Online] Available at: http://www.sudantribune.com/spip.php?article48737 [Accessed 12 December 2013]

Sudan Tribune. 2013c. *Humanitarian conditions in Darfur: A climate of violence and extreme insecurity.* [Online] Available at: http://www.sudantribune.com/spip.php?article47542 [Accessed 12 December 2013]

UN Refugee Agency, 2012. *2012 UNHCR Country Operations Profile - Sudan.* [Online] Available at: http://www.unhcr.org/pages/49e483b76.html [Accessed 14 December 2012].

UN Refugee Agency, 2012. *Dangerous Liaisons? A Historical Review of UNHCR's Engagement with Non-State Armed Actors.* [Online] Available at: http://www.unhcr.org/cgi-bin/texis/vtx/home/opendocPDFViewer.html?docid=50b62efe9andquery=darfur [Accessed 20 December 2012].

UN Refugee Agency, 2012. *UNHCR Global Appeal 2013 Central African Republic.* [Online] Available at: http://www.unhcr.org/cgi-bin/texis/vtx/home/opendocPDFViewer.html?docid=50a9f81ebandquery=darfur [Accessed 19 December 2012].

UN Refugee Agency, 2012. *UNHCR Global Appeal 2013 Update - East and Horn of Africa Subregional Overview.* [Online] Available at: http://www.unhcr.org/cgi-bin/texis/vtx/home/opendocPDFViewer.html?docid=50a9f8220andquery=darfur [Accessed 18 December 2012].

UN Refugee Agency, 2012. *UNHCR Global Appeal 2013 Update - Egypt.* [Online] Available at: http://www.unhcr.org/cgi-bin/texis/vtx/home/opendocPDFViewer.html?docid=50a9f826bandquery=darfur

UN Refugee Agency, 2012. *UNHCR Global Appeal 2013 Update - South Sudan.* [Online] Available at: http://www.unhcr.org/cgi-bin/texis/vtx/home/opendocPDFViewer.html?docid=50a9f8220andquery=darfur [Accessed 14 December 2012].

UN Refugee Agency, 2012. *UNHCR Global Appeal 2013 Update - Sudan.* [Online] Available at: http://www.unhcr.org/cgi-bin/texis/vtx/home/opendocPDFViewer.html?docid=50a9f822bandquery=darfur [Accessed 7 December 2012].

UNAMID, 2013. UNAMID peacekeepers killed, injured in South Darfur ambush. Available at http://unamid.unmissions.org/Default.aspx?tabid=11027andctl=Detailsandmid=14214andItemID=22537andlanguage=en-US.

UNHCR.2013. *2013 UNHCR country operations profile –Sudan. Working Environment.* [Online] Available at: http://www.unhcr.org/pages/49e483b76.html [Accessed 12 December 2013]

United Nations, 1945. *Charter of the United Nations.* s.l.:s.n.

United Nations, 2004. *A more Secure World: Our Shared Responsibility.* s.l.:UN.

United Nations, 2005. *Resolutions Adopted by the General Assembly: 2005 World Summit Outcome.* s.l.:s.n.

UNOCHA. 2013. *Sudan: UN Humanitarian Chief concludes visit.* [Online] Available at: http://www.unocha.org/eastern-africa/top-stories/sudan-un-humanitarian-chief-concludes-visit [Accessed 12 December 2013]

World Report. 2012. *World Report 2012: Sudan.* [Online] Available at: http://www.hrw.org/world-report-2012/world-report-2012-sudan [Accessed 12 December 2013].